FOR TRAVELERS
(AND DIGITAL NOMADS)
NOT TOURISTS:

A guide on how to connect with a destination for a more fulfilling travel experience

DANIEL V. RUSTEEN

For Travelers (and Digital Nomads) Not Tourists:
A guide on how to connect with a destination for a more fulfilling travel experience

Cover Design: Rocío Martín Osuna
Editor: Matt Sheppard
Interior Layout and Design: Jenalyn Amigable Mallari

Copyright © 2019 by Daniel V. Rusteen

All rights reserved. No part of this publication may be reproduced, stored in a retrieval system, or transmitted in any form by any means, electronic, mechanical, photocopy, recording, or otherwise, without the prior permission of the publisher, except as provided for by USA copyright law.

ISBN-13: 978-0-9997155-3-6

Custom imprinting or excerpting can also be done to fit special needs. Contact www.dannybooboo.com.

All referenced URLs and services will be available by chapter at www.dannybooboo.com/for_travelers_book

Table of Contents

1	Overview Of The Contents	1
2	Tourist Versus Traveler Versus Expat	5
3	Who Is This For—And Who Isn't It For?	7
4	Who I Am	9
5	Choosing A Location	15
	• Tier 1 Requirements	15
	» Cost Of Living	15
	» Climate	17
	» Local Population	18
	» Size	22
	» Physical Features	23
	» Digital Nomad Or Expatriate Community	24
	» Air Pollution	24
	» Visa Requirements	26
	» Transportation Or Walkability	27
	• Tier 2 Requirements	27
6	Where To Stay	31
	• Choosing The (Micro)Neighborhood	31
	• Choosing The Accommodation	39

7	What To Bring	43
	• Office	44
	• Personal	45
	• Essentials	47
	• Bathroom	49
8	What To Do Before Arrival	55
	• Flights	55
	• Maps And Places	59
	• Local Language	61
	• International And Travel Insurance	62
	• Additional Preparations	64
9	Get Acclimated Quickly (Your First Few Days)	67
10	Where To Work From	73
11	How To Make Friends And Connect	79
12	Finding Activities	89
13	How To Take Full Advantage Of Your Life	101
14	Checklist: Putting It All Together	107
15	List Of Resources	113
16	Time To Begin	115
	• Connect With Me	119

1
Overview Of The Contents

First and foremost, let's make sure this book is the right fit for you. It is not for everyone. This is covered in parts two and three. If, after reading these parts, the book is a good fit then I want to tell you about who I am and why I'm writing this book (and why you should read it) in part four.

In parts five and six, we're going to go in a roughly chronological order of how your travels will go. First, how to find destinations in the world that suit your needs and where (very specifically) to stay in your chosen destination. These two parts are of extreme importance and have the potential to make or break your trip.

In part seven, I'll tell you how to optimize what you bring with you and provide an itemized list. What

CHAPTER 1

can't you live without? What can you *definitely* live without? And what will cause an emergency if you realize at 30,000 feet that you left it in the Airbnb? You want to travel light. I'll help get you to the point where you can pack in under twenty minutes.

In part eight, we go over your pre-arrival process. You want to hit the ground running and you do this by familiarizing yourself with your new environment before you arrive. Relax, this only takes a couple hours—and you will love it because you'll know more about your destination than the local friends you are going to meet.

> Your goal is to acclimate yourself to your new environment asap.

As a bonus, if you are a gym-goer, I will have a special section on items you should (and should not) bring with you.

Part nine is all about your first few days upon arrival. Be prepared. Get acclimated. Start living like a local (and meeting them!).

Part ten is self-explanatory: where to work from. Assuming you are a long-term traveler with a source of income that you earn remotely, you will need to find places to work. As always (maybe you'll notice a pattern forming here), I have a strategy to optimize your work-travel experience.

Parts 11 and 12 guide you on how to create a fulfilling, authentic, unique travel experience, from finding out about local activities and events to making true local friends. I typically stay in a destination for about a month and I was surprised that locals actually do want to invest a significant amount of time being your friend—even though they know you will be leaving so soon. This way, you have friends all around the world who you can quite literally visit for the rest of your life.

Part 13, How To Take Full Advantage Of Your Life, challenges you to consciously think about your life instead of living it robotically. No matter where you are or what you're doing, you can find ways to maximize the time you have in this life.

My writing style is non-fluff. In preparation for this book, as I've done in the past, I read similar books that were mostly full of fluff. While this makes reading easier, it wastes time. This book is the opposite. It's dense. You will highlight a lot. If it becomes too much, know that in Part 14, Checklist – Putting It All Together, I have created a checklist summarizing everything in this book as it relates to getting to know your new destination.

CHAPTER 1

Part 15 is a complete list of resources covered throughout this book with relevant links.

Part 16, Time To Begin, shows you the criteria on how I judge a city after the month. This final score is the culmination of everything I've done based on the strategy in this book to fully experience my new destination. This helps me understand why I did or did not like a destination and to better plan out my future travels.

2

Tourist Versus Traveler Versus Expat

A **tourist** is someone who passes through a destination for less than a week. They may even change hotels midway through their stay to experience a different neighborhood. A tourist may also have a majority of their time at the destination planned out prior to arrival. And those plans typically will include mostly touristy activities. If they don't have their trip planned pre-arrival, likely they plan to find activities the day of or with a day or two of notice.

A **traveler** is someone who temporarily lives in a destination for at least two weeks. Many of their days are open so they can explore the local culture of their new destination. A traveler puts a large emphasis on making connections with the local population.

CHAPTER 2

An **expat** is someone who permanently lives in a destination for an indefinite time period. They may be there for work or because they married a local person. I find that about half actively try to make local friends and learn the local language and half make a conscious effort to stay within the expat community.

This book will be most useful to a traveler. A tourist will find a lot of value in this book. An expat will be able to use the book to better get to know their city and for their own vacations.

In any case, understand that while abroad you are an ambassador to your home country. Foreign people will attribute their experience with you to the entire country you are from. Too often I hear people talk shit about their own country. Just as it looks bad to talk shit on a prior employer or old friend, it looks equally bad to talk shit about your own country. If you truly don't like your own country, then either renounce your citizenship or do something to change it besides talking.

3

Who Is This For—And Who Isn't It For?

This book is not for everyone. I am not going to try to convince you to travel. You have to figure that out for yourself.

Instead, this book is for people wanting to make travel an integral part of their life. For me, this means traveling 365 days per year and moving to a new city every month. For you, travel may mean a couple months out of the year or even a couple weeks. Or you may prefer to be a weekend warrior, taking short and frequent trips.

It is for anyone who has felt unsatisfied after a prior vacation. The reason you felt unsatisfied is probably because you were disconnected from your travel destination. Even if you did some research before your travels (a good thing), you probably missed many gems hiding in plain sight. This book will optimize your research process before arrival, and will there optimize your time spent at the new destination.

This book is not for you if you think of an all-inclusive resort as a vacation. This book will be almost entirely useless to you.

Simply put, this book is for travelers who want a more fulfilling, authentic experience. It is going to give you the tools to take full advantage of your awesome opportunity to be living in a new destination. It is ideal for travelers who plan to spend at least two weeks per destination. You really cannot connect with the local population and make friends with a shorter stay than this.

Let's jump into a bit more about me so you can feel connected with your guide. By the way, feel free to reach me on Instagram @dannyboobooo.[1]

---

1. https://www.instagram.com/dannyboobooo/

4
Who I Am

I am a normal guy who understands how extremely fortunate he has been, but who tries to take advantage of his life in every way possible.

I was born in California and lived there for 29 years until I started indefinitely exploring the world.

I grew up slow, sexually and socially. No extreme highs or lows. I was by all accounts an average teenager. I moved away to college when I was 19 years old. Although I found high school bland as I was not popular due to my shyness, I found college a fulfilling and positive experience where I grew as a human.

I studied accounting, became a CPA, and worked in the finance industry for four years. I did not like my job. I even joined the military to get away for four months one year. I changed accounting jobs three times, eventually landing at Airbnb, who fired me almost two years to the day after they hired me.

This is when my life began.

I walked out of the San Francisco Airbnb office on that Monday evening glowing. I had just been fired, but I felt free. I was not expecting this. I felt a huge weight had lifted off my shoulders.

I was hired by a local Airbnb property management company, where I worked for a year as an operational/business development type role. And I loved it! Then I got fired—again. But it didn't matter. I'd found my calling. Business. I always knew this, but I wasn't strong enough to fire myself up and change careers while I was an accountant.

In July 2016, I started my own Airbnb property management company (www.BeloPM.com). Shortly after, I started my current online business, where I help Airbnb hosts make more money at [OptimizeMyBnb.com](http://www.optimizemybnb.com/).[1] This business fully supports my lifestyle.

---

1. http://www.optimizemybnb.com/

Through a series of realizations and conversations over the next 6 months, I decided to do a test run of the remote life in Australia. I was going to live there for three months to see if I could work remotely, make money, make friends, and, most importantly, be happy.

I had a good time, but I felt like I usually felt on vacation, the same. I did not really connect with Australia or its people. Essentially, I was just living. I did not know what I was doing. Zero planning or thinking.

Three months later, I arrived back in San Francisco unsure about my future—until three things happened to me upon my return which set me off indefinitely into the world:

1. I got a [$2,000 fine from the City of San Francisco](http://www.sfexaminer.com/airbnb-expert-fined-nearly-2k-failing-register-couch/)[2] for renting out my couch on Airbnb a year prior. I will not go into it…
2. I got a $600 fine for parking my motorcycle about one inch inside the red zone.
3. My bicycle got stolen.

Fuck this.

---
2. http://www.sfexaminer.com/airbnb-expert-fined-nearly-2k-failing-register-couch/

CHAPTER 4

No, really. Fuck this. I don't believe in destiny, but this was enough for me to say fuck it, I'm leaving. I was already halfway out anyways. I sold 90% of my belongings, became a minimalist, packed a backpack and carry-on luggage, and left for Tallinn, Estonia, with a brief stop in New York City on July 12, 2017. I have been traveling for more than two years, including my trip to Australia. [I've lived in 24 cities for at least 1 month.][3]

This book is not about how to become a digital nomad. There are plenty of resources out there on this subject (including my own below) and I believe if you really want to, you will find a way. This book is how to maximize your experiences in a foreign land.

Bonus Content: [CPA Turned Entrepreneur, My First Year][4]

I have spent anywhere from three days to three months in the same city and have found that 30 days is sufficient time to know a city. My goal is to purchase a home in the four cities that I absolutely love and make these consistent destinations each

---

3. http://www.sfexaminer.com/airbnb-expert-fined-nearly-2k-failing-register-couch/
4. https://medium.com/@DannyBooBoo/cpa-turned-entrepreneur-my-first-year-4d8a914ef70c

year while avoiding the winter year-round. I am looking for these cities now based on the strategies in this book.

I plan to live this life forever and I say that with zero hesitation in my mind. My life is better in all aspects than it was.

Here's why: Imagine working half as many hours and on your own terms.

Imagine doing this in a country that costs a fourth of what it costs to live in any major US city.

Imagine going to the grocery store or a restaurant and not worrying about the price.

Imagine walking down the street and getting looked at by attractive girls every day simply because you are exotic and different.

Imagine more easily making friends because you are now an interesting person with an awesome life.

Imagine encountering new experiences that you never would have crossed paths with living in a familiar environment.

I have grown more in the past two years than I had in the previous eight. I have made more best friends in the past two years than I had in the previous eight. I have been able to grow my business much faster by connecting with like-minded traveling entrepreneurs. I have had awesome experiences with true friends all over the world who I miss when I leave, but who I know I will return to visit.

I am fortunate and I know it. I am fortunate to know how fortunate I am. But I have also continued to put myself in a position to be fortunate.

That's me.

Oh, and my name is Daniel V. Rusteen. Nice to meet you.

5

Choosing A Location

Time is your most valuable asset, so you want to use it wisely, and that means choosing a good location, whether it be for a 10-day vacation or a few months living somewhere. Right now, I am referring to location more generally as the city. After we decide on the city, we will discuss more specifically about where to stay within a city.

Tier 1 Requirements

Cost Of Living

The biggest factor in your decision is your level of income. Based on this, you'll want to find a city with a suitable cost of living. Your cost of living is directly related to your income.

CHAPTER 5

I recommend you start with Nomad List, as it is super user friendly: **Nomad List Cost of Living**[1]

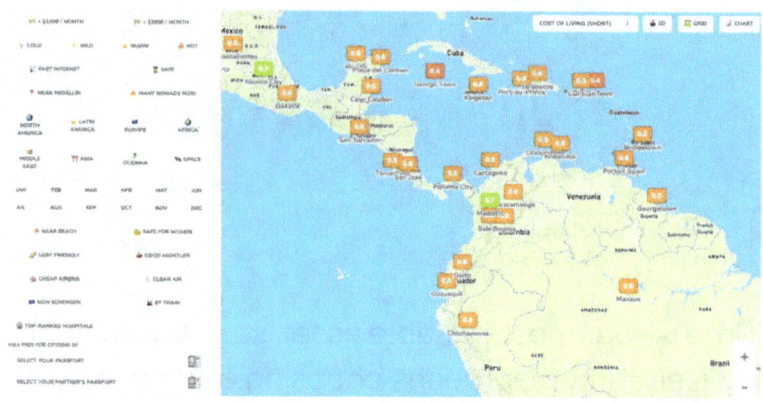

Screenshot of Nomad List City Search

There are three more resources you can use to find cities that match your current level of income/cost of living:

- **Numbeo**[2]
- **Expatistan**[3]
- **Teleport**[4]

---

1. https://nomadlist.com/cost-of-living
2. https://www.numbeo.com/cost-of-living/
3. https://www.expatistan.com/cost-of-living
4. https://teleport.org/

Choosing A Location

> **TIP**
>
> If a city's cost of living is a bit too high, but you really want to go, travel during the low season.

No matter who you are, cost of living will narrow your options down significantly.

Climate

This requirement will equally narrow your options.

You already know if you prefer cold or warm or rainy or dry. With this information, you will use the following website to further narrow down what city you may want to explore: https://goo.gl/So1hsB[5]

A really useful dataset I found to narrow down your search by major criteria.

---

5. https://goo.gl/So1hsB

At this point, as shown above, you will have narrowed down your choices to zones. In the image above, the user prefers warm weather in January (see dials on the right). Assuming your level of income was on the lower side, you would be able to easily rule out Australia, Brazil, Argentina, New Zealand, South Africa, and a few Asian countries like Hong Kong, Japan, and Singapore.

However, even within expensive cities, there are ways to live well below the cost of living. But this will diminish your experience and I recommend you not start in a city with a cost of living above your current level. After all, living in a 12-bed hostel on the outskirts of the city, cooking your own ramen, and walking everywhere is going to affect your ability to optimize your experience!

I digress: that leaves a portion of North, Central and South America (nearly all of Latin America, in other words), Africa, South East Asia, and India. Not too shabby!

Local Population

This is subjective, but there are three facets you may want to consider:

1. Are you attracted to the men or women?
2. Are the locals friendly?

3. Do they speak English? (That is, if you don't plan to learn the local language—which, in fact, I highly recommend you do!)

Question one is very straightforward, and will only be important to you if you are single and believe that experiences with the opposite sex in a romantic way would enhance your own experience. If you are attracted to Asian women, well, you are going to Asia. If you like Latin women, well, you probably want to go to Latin America.

Question two is quite murky. For me, the friendliness of locals is a giant factor in my liking a city or not. However, I realized something while talking with a friend from Indonesia. Stockholm ranks as one of the friendliest places I have ever visited. Every interaction I had with strangers, including with a team of street cops, was incredibly friendly. But this friend passionately disagrees. Based on his personal experiences there, he felt it was quite an unfriendly place. Why such a drastic difference of opinions?

I believe it is due to different internal values. I will explain this with an example. Let's assume an atheist goes to a country where they value religion more than most. If this is true, it would make sense that this person may have a hard time connecting with locals, men or women. Many of the social activities may be centered around religion, as would daily life. He probably will attribute it to the people, which I suppose it is. But, really, it is a mismatch of values. If you asked this person what they thought, they would steer you away from this hypothetical location. But if you asked a religious person the same question, they may enthusiastically tell you about the culture and the interesting local customs.

Religion is an obvious reason why you may or may not like a city, but the point is that the person may not realize that some of the inner values they hold lead them to like or dislike a city. And these inner values are different for everyone.

Essentially what I am saying is whether a person liked or disliked a city is so subjective that you should not even ask. Instead ask them what their least favorite or most favorite part was and identify how important their answer will be for your own situation.

> Different values is why one person loves a city and another hates it.

Regardless, question two above should definitely be important to you if you are reading this book. Unfortunately, we don't know if the locals will be friendly towards you, but there are generalities you can take from the internet. Some cultures tend to be more friendly and open than others. In Morocco you might be invited to lunch with a family you meet on the street, while in Russia you might find it hard to make eye contact with anyone. There are exceptions, but the generalizations come from somewhere.

In some places, the locals are simply not open. It's not necessarily a bad thing, depending on what you are after. For example, I noticed the people from Tallinn, in Estonia, were particularly closed-off to strangers. I'm sure if you got to know them they are very friendly, but if it is hard to get to know someone, that creates a large block. They do not smile or engage in any small talk, which I did not like and made it hard to connect.

Right about now, you should tell me to eat shit.

Why?

Because I just told you my opinion of a place. It is just my opinion. While there are generalities, do not take them at face value. While I was not able to connect with the people of Estonia, maybe it was my personality? Maybe you have the perfect personality and you would go there and make friends so easily you wouldn't believe it. It's possible. The key is to gain knowledge, and with more travel experience you will be able to apply what you learned in prior cities to future cities.

Size

A simple google search will tell you the city size, but there are a few things to keep in mind. If a city is 600k, but there are no cities around it, it is going to feel smaller than a city of 600k with another city of 600k right next to it. For example, I am from Redwood City, California, with a population of 85,000. However, for miles and miles and miles each city starts and ends one after another. The population of the San Francisco metropolitan area is almost 5,000,000 and spans no more than 25 miles. In other words, when you're in Redwood City, you feel like you're in a much bigger city.

On the other hand, the population of Pereira, Colombia is 500,000 but the next closest city is one hour away. So it almost feels the same size as Redwood City.

If you are like me and prefer bigger cities, then this narrows down your options significantly as you will only have one option in many countries and only two or three in many more.

> **TIP**
>
> For a more authentic experience, go to the 2nd or 3rd largest city. This works best in first world countries where these cities will still have all of the modern conveniences. However, remember, the more "authentic" means the less English will be spoken. It will be hard to connect without being able to effectively communicate.

Physical Features

This one is a piece of cake. Do you prefer the beach or the mountains, or somewhere in between? Does the city have what you want, or is it near enough to what you want that it doesn't matter? In Granada, in southern Spain, for example, you can be skiing in the Sierra Nevada in half an hour from the center of the city, and you can be swimming in the Mediterranean 45 minutes in the other direction. Look into the physical features of a city and its surroundings. It's worth it.

CHAPTER 5

Digital Nomad Or Expatriate Community

These can easily be found with Nomad List. Generally, but not always, it will be a larger city. For example, Chiang Mai, Thailand, is arguably the biggest digital nomad hub in the world, yet the population is less than 200,000. Later in the book, we will figure out where the expat zone is within your chosen city, if that's where you want to stay.

Air Pollution

At first, this wasn't an important metric for me. Being from a first world city, this was not even a thought of mine. And, going on a week vacation somewhere, it will not be of big concern. But when you have to walk by a bus ten times per day spewing black crude, you start to wonder. In Medellin, Colombia

Exhaust of many buses in Central and South America.

there are government mandated days when you can and cannot drive based on your license plate number. There are also days without cars. This can be inconvenient. This city is also in a valley, so all the air pollution just sits there and builds up.

Anything above 50 measured with PM10 is polluted and anything below 20 is acceptable. Additionally, you can look up that cities AQI (Air Quality Index) most of the time with an easy search. I find the best website and highest search result is https://aqicn.org/[6].

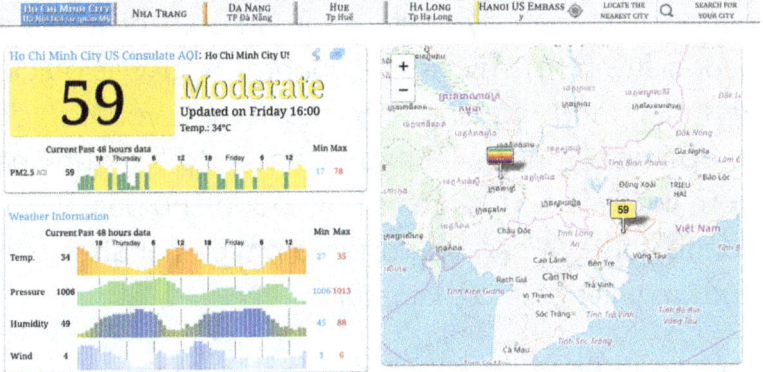

AQI for Ho Chi Minh City. This number changes by the hour, sometimes drastically. In the past 24 hours, the AQI has went from 17 to 78.

---

6. https://aqicn.org/

CHAPTER 5

Visa Requirements

As an American, this is of very low importance to me because I'm either allowed visa-free or pay a tax upon arrival into 163 countries. For you, this experience may differ. The factor to take into consideration here is the easiness of the visa. If it's very easy to get a visa, well, then there is no administration time needed on your part to enter, which is very hassle-free. The downside is that there will be more tourists there, especially from your home country.

At first, I ignored any country that required a visa application, reasoning that there are plenty that do not. But now I realize that those countries with visa requirements actually create a more authentic experience for me by limiting the amount of tourists, especially from my home country. You will quickly understand the single greatest thing you can do to optimize your travel experience is to look unique from the locals. This draws both good and bad attention to you. We can optimize both types of attention, and we will get into that later.

The countries with strict visa requirements usually have a lower cost of living. And your foreigner value skyrockets. Foreigner value is how easy it is to create connections, both romantically and platonically, with locals just due to the fact that you are a foreigner.

Transportation Or Walkability

I do not take into consideration walkability or transportation because of two reasons:

1. There is always a neighborhood that is walkable to most, if not all, of your daily or weekly errands (grocery store, gym, park, café, etc.) and this where I choose to live.
2. Ride sharing services like Uber, Grab, Lyft, etc.

However, later, when we decide on the neighborhood, this will become more of a factor.

Tier 2 Requirements

The Tier 2 requirements basically supersede Tier 1 requirements, but they are all related to special circumstances. For example, if you want to go to Fuji Rock (a music concert in the jungle of Japan) in July and you prefer a dry climate… well, your Tier 2 requirement just superseded every one of your Tier 1 requirements.

If you are traveling to obtain a skill, you will want to go to the city in the world within your budget where it is most efficient to learn that skill. If you want to learn Spanish, there are a handful of cities where it is best to do this. Even if you prefer the beach, you would strongly consider Antigua, Guatemala, because of the hundreds of schools within a six-block radius and the neutral and slower Spanish the locals speak—and because the English proficiency is not super high (many teachers do not even speak English!), giving you more opportunity to practice. On top of that, it is a super walkable city and the cost of living is extremely cheap. If you can't tell, I love Antigua.

(If learning languages is of interest to you, check out my book [Zilch to Conversational: A Guide to Quickly Attain Conversational Fluency in Any Language](http://www.dannybooboo.com/zilch_to_conversational))[7]

However, if you wanted to learn Salsa, you would strongly consider Cali, Colombia, a city of 2.5 million, even if you prefer smaller cities.

If there is a conference that happens once a year, this will supersede all else. This is a great reason to travel, especially if you have a specific skill or conference you want to go to, as you can meet like-minded travelers, which is one of the best ways to connect.

---

7. http://www.dannybooboo.com/zilch_to_conversational

To start you off, here is a list of neat conferences (many are geared towards the digital nomad type):

Nomad Train — 18-day trans-Siberian train crossing Russia to China.

Nomad Cruise — 7-10 day cruise held 3 times per year.

DCBKK — Annual 6-day conference in Bangkok, Thailand, full of higher-level entrepreneurs.

> **TIP**
>
> **Bonus Destination Tip – Consider the Season**
>
> All destinations have a busy season in line with their best weather. The pros of this—besides the weather itself—is that there will be more events and nothing will be closed. However, there are a lot more downsides with travel during busy season:
> - More expensive flights and accommodations.
> - Longer lines, busier streets and public transit, crowded bars and restaurants, etc.
> - Less authentic experience (due to more tourists, locals less willing to interact).

> **High On Life** — Annual tantra festival in Tallin, Estonia.
>
> **Airbnb Open** — Semi-annual gathering of Airbnb hosts and guests held on a different continent.
>
> **Aventura Dance Cruise** — 3-5 day cruise for dancers of Latin music.

To be clear, I am not advocating travel during your destination's off-season. The downsides of off-season travel are plentiful. For one, there will be fewer events and activities. Venues could simply be closed. In Casablanca, Morocco, I walked to a pool-party venue with a bunch of stellar reviews only to show up and it be closed because it was low season. I was there in November, which was low season, but the weather was still warm (just not as warm as busy season in this destination). The flip side is the opposite of the above list: less expensive flights and accommodations, more authentic experiences, and less crowds, which leads to a bunch of other benefits.

6
Where To Stay

Choosing The (Micro)Neighborhood

After you decide what city you want to travel to, you will need to decide which neighborhood to stay in and, specifically, which section of that neighborhood. This is of extreme importance because you will likely be using your feet or public transit for most transport. If you choose a neighborhood without any public transit nearby and far from grocery stores, bars, cafés, and gyms, you are going to have to spend more time walking or more money on Ubers or taxis. Additionally, because you will be using your feet most of the time, you will want to be walking in a neighborhood that you enjoy.

CHAPTER 6

This is more of an art than a science because one neighborhood is not right for everyone. Personally, I prefer central areas where I can walk to everything. If you want a younger demographic, then maybe you search for the largest universities in the city. My first stop will be a simple google search of neighborhoods in my selected city (search 'popular (or hipster or trendy or party, etc.) neighborhoods [city]'). Certain things will pop out at you that you should make note of. For example, if a neighborhood says it is for families, I can rule this out. Based on my reading of the relevant articles, I will usually be able to narrow my search down to two or three neighborhoods at this point.

The smaller the city, the easier this will be. In Chiang Mai, a small city, there was really only one neighborhood I kept seeing, Nimman.

Larger cities like Manila, in the Philippines, will have many options. In Manila's case, there are five cities smack next to Manila, taking the metropolitan area population to 13 million. You could choose to stay in Cubao, Quezon City or Makati, Manila. These two neighborhoods are in two different cities and only 7 miles apart, but it would take you over an hour to travel between the two due to traffic. Or, you would choose to stay in BGC, just east of Makati, but not within walking distance.

The newest, up-and-coming neighborhoods will be extremely hard to find as the internet is usually a couple years behind, unless you are able to find that hidden gem blog. In Bangkok, Thailand, I choose to stay in Silom, but when I arrived, I found Thong Lor, which was a new neighborhood East of the main areas. As the city keeps expanding, newer neighborhoods pop up further East.

Alternatively, the recommended neighborhoods could be the favorites of yesteryear. My online research about Guatemala City indicated that Zona Viva was the nicer area with many bars, restaurants, and café's. Upon arrival, I discovered that Zona Rosa was the place to be about 10 years prior and had been slowly falling out of popularity year by year ever since. It's something to be cognizant of during your research.

The same will be true of highly recommended bars, cafes, and restaurants. Leopold's Café was highly recommended via the internet in the Colaba district of Mumbai, India. The description made it seem like a hip café with a calm vibe where both tourists and Bollywood celebrities hang out. When I visited, I

CHAPTER 6

Leopold's Cafe in the Colaba district of Mumbai, India

saw tables smashed together like a university dining commons to take advantage of the all the willing tourists and a hectic vibe.

Another strategy to make use of is setting your Tinder location to your chosen city and asking a dozen matches what neighborhood they live in. Statistics say you will find the most popular/populous neighborhoods. From there, you can ask your match to recommend you a neighborhood based on a few criteria. As they live there, it can be a really helpful resource. As with the difference in opinions we talked about above, this is just one piece of information, so don't put too much weight in it. But at the very least, you may form a friendship or something more!

After you decide on your neighborhood, sometimes you will encounter micro-neighborhoods. Depending on the size of the neighborhood, that could mean a 20-minute or more walk. That is, 20 minutes each way at least once per day. To demonstrate, let me tell you about Medellin, Colombia. The most popular neighborhood is El Poblado, but the neighborhood is actually quite large. You can dig a bit more to find out that Parque Lleras is the party district or that Provenza is bordered with Parque Lleras, but is the higher-end, mellower part. Additionally, you could choose Manila, a much mellower, cheaper neighborhood within a 10-minute walk to Parque Lleras.

I find that within a 10-minute walk of the main area is ideal.

Likely, you will want to be near nightlife as you will not want to walk as far at night when you go out. I do not go out more than once every other week, but I still prefer to be near the nightlife so that in case I do go out people are coming towards my area. It is also more convenient for evening dates. One of my searches to narrow down my specific location is 'best areas to stay for nightlife [city]'.

It can be extremely difficult to find exactly where you want to stay in a neighborhood, but there are a couple guidelines if you want to be near a convenient area:

1. Near large shopping malls is usually a good bet.

2. After you do your research on the area, save the locations you are interested in to your map. This will tell you where you will be spending most of your time.

3. The yellow-tinted zones on Google maps indicate high foot traffic areas. However, this does not always mean shopping, cafés, and bars. See below for a map from Cali, Colombia. The larger zone to the right was actually an industrial zone selling furniture and the smaller zone to the left was where the park, bars, shopping, cafés, and restaurants were at. So zoom in on these zones to ensure a bunch of cafés, bars, and restaurants pop up.

Where To Stay

4. Near parks
5. Near public transit lines like the metro. See below for an image of the Skyrail transit lines in Bangkok and note the amount of yellow-tinted areas (and shopping centers) near the transit spots.

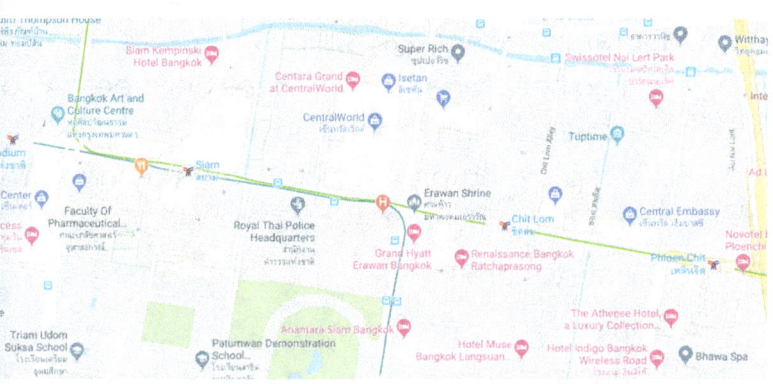

Or maybe you couldn't care less about nightlife? The thing is, this book is how *I* travel, so please read it with that frame of mind. Everything may not be for you, but at least you will start thinking of these things sooner. With that in mind, here is how I choose my micro-neighborhood, in order of preference:

1. Nearby gym options
    a. I go to the gym 3-5 days per week, more than any of my other routines. Also, I look for many gyms because that indicates it is a high foot traffic area, which is my preference.
2. Bars
    a. I will go out to party with friends once every other week, but I will also go to happy hours with friends or on dates. This takes preference because when I do, I do not want to have to travel far at night.
3. Libraries, coworking spaces, or cafés
    a. I go here three or four times per week. Also signifies high foot traffic area.
    b. Depending on your city you may need to be near an internet café.
4. Grocery store
5. Park
6. Laundromat

Choosing The Accommodation

If you decide to go the shared-room hostel route, ensure there are private in-room lockers (and bring your own lock). Also ensure there is in-room wi-fi (sometimes it is only free or provided in the common areas). Find out how many beds are in the hostel. Generally, the more beds, the more of a party hostel you will get, which means the louder and dirtier the common areas are. Check www.Hostelz.com[1] as it is a comparison site for all the hostels. Search in reviews for terms like 'solo travel' or 'travelling alone' to read relevant reviews. Hostels are a fine option for short-term travel when you do not have professional commitments (i.e. a vacation). As an introvert, I find hostels overwhelming. I started my full-time travel life in hostels, but switched to Airbnb within a few months.

[Airbnb](http://www.airbnb.com/c/drusteen)[2] is the best option and will almost always be better than a hotel. You can find cheap hostels or you can find entire homes with a full kitchen. Having a kitchen to cook my meals is one of the things that make long-term travel doable for me. While it can be more expensive to use Airbnb, the convenience

---
1. http://www.Hostelz.com
2. http://www.airbnb.com/c/drusteen

is like nothing else. Plus, you have no extra bills to pay for (phone, trash, water, electricity, internet are all included). You will find your must-haves out for yourself quickly. To find better deals, go towards the end of search results, as these are new hosts. If you find a host with anything below a 4.5-star average, read the reviews. Often times you can spot a deal just because a prior guest left a bad review. Here is a message I send while searching in a new city:

"Hi **[host name]** – I am an experienced guest with over 600 nights on Airbnb, Superhost, non-smoker, and author of "Optimize YOUR Airbnb". I used to work at Airbnb! I'm reaching out to my top 3 Airbnbs in the area and will decide where I stay based on our conversation. If you are flexible with your nightly rate, I'm grateful. I run a business where I help Airbnb hosts make more money. My stay will include a video review."

Notice that I am indirectly asking for a discount. I only send this to hosts where I am staying for at least 2 weeks. Obviously, you will want to tweak it. For example, if you won't use the kitchen, say so. Or, if you will be at a conference all day every day, say so, because it means you will not be using the Airbnb.

Once you start to figure out what cities you want to return to on a regular basis, you will want to get in touch with building management and work out a deal. For example, you can search for furnished apartment buildings. The monthly prices on Airbnb are two to three times higher than a local tenant, even if that local tenant is renting on a monthly basis like you.

If you are less concerned about location, I recommend Facebook groups. The availability will be limited as compared to hostels or Airbnbs, but the pricing will be much cheaper. Try searching "[city] housing" or "expat housing [city]". When I've used this method, even if I did not end up renting a home from a listing on Facebook, often times I become friends with some of the people who reach out about my inquiry. It's always welcomed to arrive at a new destination with a local friend already in your contact list.

You can also search "long term hotels/housing [city]" on google. Ask the local language schools where they recommend their students stay as they are usually coming for many months.

If you are only in a city for a few nights, then you can do the hotel option. I recommend Priceline Express Deals or the HotelTonight app.

7

What To Bring

I'll ignore obvious things like a computer or underwear, unless I have a specific recommendation or tip.

As a general rule, remember to always bring extra cash with you to the airport to be exchanged in the new country upon arrival. I used to never do this, opting to tip the taxi driver the remainder of my local cash upon getting to the airport, until I got caught in 95-degree weather cashless and signal-less in Bangkok. That was a worst case scenario, but I arrived in Bangkok without any cash, assuming I could Uber to my hotel. Not possible as they use Grab. Instead my best/cheaper option was to take a local bus with cash-only payments. (I did not want to sign up for Grab at the airport as the bus left every 5 minutes.) Well, my bank blocked my debit card, but the bus driver let me board anyways. Well, the nice driver told me to get off at the wrong stop. My phone usually takes a while to connect in a new country and so I was without cash, without a phone signal, without a way to get cash, and somewhere in Bangkok. Taxi was my only option, but they don't accept credit card. Needless to say, this wasn't a pleasant afternoon and could have been solved had I carried just $20 in extra cash with me.

Office

- [Roost Stand][1]
    - » It's expensive, but it's the best in terms of quality, craftsmanship, and weight. I've had mine for 3 years.
- [Extra monitor][2]
- Bluetooth trackpad and keyboard
    - » Avoid extra wires whenever possible.
- External hard drive
    - » You could also backup to a cloud storage system like iCloud.
- Business cards
- Apple Bluetooth earpods

---

1. https://amzn.to/2C49ox2
2. https://amzn.to/2C49fbq

> **TIP**
>
> Place a fragile sticker on your luggage, which means you are the last to be loaded and first to be unloaded, in addition, it requires staff to be more gentle. The way I got my sticker (which has stayed on my carry-on for over a year) was to check it once and simply tell the counter agent I had camera equipment inside, which was enough for them to slap two giant red fragile stickers on each side of my luggage.

Personal

- [Portable outdoor beach chair][3]
  - This thing is great! Can be a chair, a pillow, or a back rest for the park or a beach.

- [Kindle Voyager][4]
  - This model is actually the smallest on the market, but a bit harder to find. It's better than the recently released paperwhite.

---

[3]: https://amzn.to/2RCtBCm
[4]: https://amzn.to/2C0flEq

- [Flat-style wallet](#) [5]
    - » I'm not sure why these have never caught on over the bulky traditional wallets, but this one has been with me for over 12 years compliments of my Dad (it was a gift)
- Selfie stick + tripod
    - » This really comes in handy if you do any video for your online business.
- Bucket hat
- Lightweight, foldable backpack
    - » I got mine in Sydney, Australia, from an outdoor shop.

> **TIP**
>
> Virtual Sim Card applications can be useful for local numbers as you sometimes will need one. The one I use is Numero, but a quick search will bring up many options.

---

5. https://amzn.to/2CAzBTv

Essentials

- International power adapter
- Mini foam pillow
    - » Absolute essential for making uncomfortable chairs, airplane or bus seats 10x more comfy.
- Eye cover
- Ear plugs
- Debit cards that refund ATM fees
    - » Start with your credit union first or Charles Schwab.
- Credit cards without international fees
    - » Most already do this, but ensure there is no fee in the conversation rate which should be the true rate.
- Note: Bring all physical debit and credit cards (or a high-quality photo) in case you get locked out of any accounts.
- External phone battery
    - » Anything above 5,000mAh gets too big to easily carry.
- International license
    - » If in the US, available at AAA.

- A few $100 bills in USD
  - » For emergencies. As USD is the most common currency, almost everyone will accept it.
  - » In some countries (like Uzbekistan), exchanging USD actually will get you 2x the rate.
- Stain remover stick
- [Inflatable neck pillow](https://amzn.to/2CwZm7r) [6]
  - » This combined with eye mask, ear plug, and mini pillow allows you to sleep upright in airplanes and buses just like you are in your bed.
- [Reach floss pick](https://amzn.to/2C04otx) [7]
  - » Even if you do not travel, you should still get this as it is 100x better than floss.
- Shoes
  - » I use converse or something, both super lightweight and flexible. I carry one pair of slippers, sandals, trainers (for the gym, running, hiking, playing basketball) and casual shoes.

---

6. https://amzn.to/2CwZm7r
7. https://amzn.to/2C04otx

TIP

Purchase a VPN service which will allow you to access your favorite sites (like Netflix and Facebook) in countries with restrictions. Additionally, the content on Netflix changes based on your country. I use and recommend Ivacy which has a solid phone app, too.

Bathroom

- Mini shaver
    - » Cordless is ideal with batteries.
- Eye drops
- [Beard comb][8]
- [Natural salt deodorant][9]
    - » I get the one for females because it is smaller. They are made of identical ingredients and it will last you 6+ months. Just be sure to apply more than once per day!

---

8. https://amzn.to/2CQMd9E
9. https://amzn.to/2C6rfls

- **[Neutrogena Rapid Clear Acne Eliminating Spot Gel](#)**[10]
  - » If you think you have a zit coming, use this and it is gone every time the next day. It is magical.
- **[Manual nose trimmer](#)**[11]
  - » I have used this for 5+ years. Also magical.
- **[Travel-sized nail clippers with nail cleaner pick](#)**[12]
  - » Keep the smallest and gift the other three. It is hard to find travel-sized clippers with the swing out nail cleaner.
- **[Dr. Bronner's 18-in-1 soap](#)**[13]
  - » This is a super-condensed soap. I use it for shampoo and body wash. You only need a few drops. When the bottle depletes by 25%, just fill it up with water.
- Toothpaste (no more than a 100g tube which will last 5 weeks)

---

10. https://amzn.to/2LQwg6m
11. https://amzn.to/2C5KDiO
12. https://amzn.to/2SFfPwc
13. https://amzn.to/2CPwtE3

> » No matter how inconsequential a 150g tube seems, I urge you to always be vigilant in keeping volume to a minimum as they add up. Believe it or not, I have a friend who rides a motorcycle around the world and brings along a printer and a giant-size cologne bottle. I bet it all started with that oversized toothpaste tube! :D

Not only is the gym the single best thing you can do for your health and longevity, but you can also meet locals here. Tourists do not go to the gym. Here is what you need:

- Lightweight microfiber towel
  - » A towel can take up a lot of room in your luggage, but this one is super lightweight. You do not need a size larger than 16x32 inches (40x80cm). Buy it at any travel goods or backpacker store.
- [Gripads weightlifting gloves](https://amzn.to/2LRv5Ub)[14]
  - » I found these a few years ago and, in addition to being lightweight and small, they are also just better than regular gloves.

---

14. https://amzn.to/2LRv5Ub

- [Gym bag][15]
    » Lightweight with zipper for your wallet and wrist rubber bands.
- [IronMind wrist rubber bands][16]
    » Also serves as a game for your friends to see who has the strongest wrists.
- [Wide-mouth shaker][17]
    » Wide-mouth lets you clean it without a special tool. This is the standard, though I buy a better stainless steel shaker at GNC.

You are going to lose things. It will happen. To avoid the larger headaches, you want to make a list of things that you absolutely, 100% cannot forget without causing an emergency. To ensure I have everything, I will bold each item in my google document upon packing when it reaches the inside of my luggage. For me, these items are:

- Debit card (I only have one)
- Massage tool (irreplaceable and super useful)
- Retainer (expensive and hard to get)

---

15. https://amzn.to/2AyNX5M
16. https://amzn.to/2VwgPog
17. https://amzn.to/2CQOEsO

- Passport
- External battery (the one I have is really tiny for the output it gives and has iPhone, android, and microSD ports making it really useful)
- Computer
- External monitor (I use this daily and would significantly hurt my productivity and it's hard to get)
- International charger (The one I have is perfect, slim, fast charging, and all-in-one)
- You will want to add any specialty chargers or cords to this list

8

What To Do Before Arrival

Flights

Obviously, you will want to purchase your flight before arrival. Unless you are an expert in finding cheap fares, I recommend using Flystein. Essentially, they will search on your behalf. They really become worth it for flights in excess of $1,000 because they can save you $200+ or they refund your money. I have used them a handful of times and only once they refunded my money because their deal was not much better than the one I found myself.

If you want to be a little more hands on, I hesitatingly (see below) recommend two tools:

- [Travel Hacking Cartel](http://travelhacking.org/DRUSTY87-WANTS-YOU)[1] – They help you earn points. I have been a member off-and-on since 2010.
- [Scott's Cheap Flights](https://scottscheapflights.com/)[2] – They find cheap flights from your selected airport to your preferred destinations.

Or, if you simply want to search on your own, I find the following tools to be the best. However, I also find that spending hours searching for the cheapest flight is no longer worth your time. Pretty much all the search engines are showing you the same things and if you happen to find what looks to be a deal on one website, you will probably find it on another. Save your time and either book something quick or hire the experts above:

- [Google Flights](https://www.google.com/flights)[3]
- [Skiplagged](https://skiplagged.com/)[4] – This company finds you cheaper deals by finding flights where your destination is a layover instead of the final stop. United Airlines sued this company over their strategies, but they lost. Downside is because

---

1. http://travelhacking.org/DRUSTY87-WANTS-YOU
2. https://scottscheapflights.com/
3. https://www.google.com/flights
4. https://skiplagged.com/

the airlines are aware of this, you are not going to find many killer deals that you will not find on the other search engines, but it is very user-friendly.
- [Adioso](https://adioso.com/)[5] – This one is super cool because you can search more broadly with your dates and destinations.

Finally, you only have to be caught on a Scoot Airlines flight back row without reclining seats, next to the bathroom, and without a window once to start using [Seat Guru](https://www.seatguru.com/)[6]. If you book with an airline that lets you choose your seat (free or otherwise), give this site a quick search to optimize your decision.

Travel hacking is a waste of time. After about 10 years of a love-hate relationship with this time-wasting hobby, I have finally come to peace with how useless it really is. The investment of time does not justify the savings on airfare. It takes so much time to learn how to properly travel hack then to vet credit cards, airlines you use, alliances, miscellaneous offers, etc. For what? To get status on an airline that you have to maintain? No thanks. I'll spend that time building my business or improving myself.

---

5. https://adioso.com/
6. https://www.seatguru.com/

CHAPTER 8

In the past, travel hacking was real and effective, but it's well past its golden years. Just as Skiplagged used to be awesome until the airlines figured it out, the same thing happened to travel hacking. The airlines are well aware of the travel hacking community and employ teams to ensure 99% waste their time.

In an effort to hopefully save thousands of readers hours, let me plead my case.

You have two options. First is to use a tool above or search for your own flights and simply book one of the cheaper flights. Second is to travel hack. The process of travel hacking requires hours of learning how to travel hack. Then you will register with the various airline rewards programs, sign up for a tool to track all of your travel hacking activity (none of these tools work with some of the major airlines rewards programs), sign up for numerous 'travel hacking' tools (all which cost money). Then, you will figure out that you can only use a select few airlines in order to earn points. And guess what? These select providers are almost always more expensive with less flight options.

And for the grand finale, any of these reward programs can devalue their points at any moment, as happens often.

Regardless, if you really want to travel hack and have dozens of hours available to you to get started and for ongoing continuing education, then I do believe there are some hacks you'll discover. I just don't think the time investment is worth it nor enjoyable.

Maps And Places

Next, download the google map of your city to your phone for use while you are not connected to wi-fi. You can only do this while you are connected to wi-fi. The setting you want to click is called 'Maps without connection'.

To maximize your time, there are some things you can do before your arrival—like on the flight or while you wait to board your flight. First, save certain destinations that you know you will search for anyways on your map ahead of time. I save these destinations in relation to my accommodation as I plan to walk for the majority of the time. These are:

- Coworking spaces
- Libraries
- Cafés (search also coffee shop)
- Gyms (search also health club, or fitness club)

- Grocery store (search also supermarket)
- Shopping centers
- Laundromat
- Bars and restaurants
  » We will cover this when I tell you how to research a new destination as you will likely have a handful of these already saved.
- Anything miscellaneous. For me, this would be a supplement store.

Find out three things (activity, cuisine, etc.) a country or city is known for and immerse yourself in this to get in touch with the local culture and meet local residents. You can search for 'interesting facts [city]'. Some examples are Muay Thai in Thailand, coffee in Guatemala, salsa in Colombia, or basketball in the Philippines. If you are traveling to a destination already visited by me, I may have this already answered for you. See my article on Medium titled "[City Impression from a Digital Nomad](#) [7]". You can use this information to search for activity-based events to further meet people, but we will get into that later.

---

[7]. https://medium.com/@DannyBooBoo/capital-city-impressions-from-a-digital-nomad-29045cdecf05

Local Language

I recommend you learn a bit of the language. It is interesting to note that some cultures are more or less open to you speaking their native tongue, but I always learn the basics no matter where I go, no matter how hard the language is. If I am someplace for a month, I am usually learning about 50 words or phrases. This sets me apart from 95% of tourists who learn either nothing or just 'hello' and 'thank you'. It also gives the locals a good laugh if you can pick up some good slang words.

Download [Anki](...)[8] to basically memorize anything, but it is super useful in terms of learning languages. I wrote a detailed article on how to use this app on Medium: "[A Step-by-Step Guide to Learning Any Language Efficiently Based on "Fluent Forever" by Gabriel Wyner](...)[9]".

Here is a list of common words you will want to know in your target language:

- Hello
- Please

---

8. https://www.ankiapp.com/
9. https://medium.com/@DannyBooBoo/quick-summary-of-fluent-forever-by-gabriel-wyner-step-by-step-guide-to-learning-any-language-7f150613e5d0

- Thank you
- Bye
- Yes and no
- Good morning/afternoon/evening
- Bathroom
- Water
- Cool (usually there is a slang way to say this)
- What?
- How are you?
- You're welcome
- Excuse me
- Right, left, stop, straight
- How much?
- Your preferred meat (chicken, etc.)
- You're cute.
- What's your name?

International And Travel Insurance

You will want to get either international health insurance or additional travel insurance. For travel insurance (something shorter term), I recommend World Nomads[10]. If you want international health

---

10. https://www.worldnomads.com/Turnstile/AffiliateLink?partnerCode=booboo&utm_source=booboo&source=weblink&utm_content=weblink&path=https://www.worldnomads.com

insurance (long-term), go with [GeoBlue](https://www.geo-blue.com/)[11]. While it is true that this is a personal choice, I did quite a bit of research on this (three full day's worth) and I decided on GeoBlue because of the amount of benefits offered compared to price and existing online reviews. In the year I've had them, I had made claims and been reimbursed quickly. Additionally, they will make the appointment on your behalf so you do not need to pay out of pocket. Their customer phone support is superb.

Actually, I posted my results on Nomad List over 2 years ago and I still get weekly emails asking me about my results. I will post an excel document for download at the book website at www.dannybooboo.com/fortravellersbook.

Another option, which I have not used, is Safety Wing. They market themselves for traveling or location-independent digital nomads and entrepreneurs. Their plans are competitively priced.

If you are carrying lots of photography equipment, I highly recommend getting separate insurance for your electronic and photo gear. Check out Pho-

---

[11]. https://www.geo-blue.com/

toguard, which lets you build your insurance based on the value of your exact set of equipment.

The best resource for international health and prevention, including recommended vaccines, can be found at https://wwwnc.cdc.gov/travel/destinations/list/.[12]

Additional Preparations

Where appropriate, you will want to change your current city to reflect the one you are about to travel to. Some examples of where this will be appropriate is Facebook, Internations (I will tell you what this is in Chapter 10: How to Make Friends and Connect), Couchsurfing, and Meetup.com. Doing this allows you to views relevant events in that city.

You will want to join relevant Facebook groups based on your interests and hobbies. For me, I join groups about digital nomads, expats, Latin/salsa dancing, language exchanges, and Americans (usually 'Americans in [city]').

---

12. https://wwwnc.cdc.gov/travel/destinations/list/

If you do not have a permanent address in your home country, you'll want to get a temporary one where someone, typically a business, collects your mail and sends it to you. There are many mail forwarding and virtual addresses to choose from. To make your life easier, I recommend [Earth Class Mail](https://www.earthclassmail.com/).[13] To be frank, you will find some unhappy customers, but they've been around the longest, are affordable, and easy to work with.

---

13. https://www.earthclassmail.com/

9

Get Acclimated Quickly (Your First Few Days)

The following activities I do within the first week of arrival in order to maximize my time at the new destination. Additionally, any time I am outside walking around, I ensure I am doing two things: First, I want to be keeping an eye out for anything cool (event advertisements, food parks, etc.). Second, I want to look for people who I can enter into conversation with in order to make local connections. For me, making local connections is directly related to whether or not I enjoy a city. And it brings me out of my comfort zone, which I prefer.

In order of chronological importance, I will do the following within the first five days. First, I will **visit the tourist information center** or tour agency. I am

CHAPTER 9

searching for activities and day trips. Search google maps for 'travel agency', 'tour agency', and 'tourist info center'.

Next, I **visit the saved locations** on my map. In the process of doing other things, if you are nearby a café or park, go check it out. Often you won't spend more than 30 seconds at a saved location before you realize you do not like it and unsave it from your map.

Next, if you plan to cook, then you will be making frequent trips to the grocery store. I suggest you **sign up for the grocery store loyalty card** as many places apply discounts to card holders. If you do not, then every time you check out, use this as a tool for conversation by asking the person behind or in front of you if they would like to earn your points. They will just give their number or card to the cashier before she starts to ring you up.

On a side note, while you are in the grocery store, take this as an opportunity to make connections. In fact, **take everything as an opportunity to make connections**. Not sure what fruit you are looking at? Or if it is ripe? Or sweet or sour? Or maybe you cannot find the peanut butter? Go ahead and ask a shopper for help and maybe that conversation turns into a friend. You'd be surprised how often a conversation follows from a simple question in a foreign land. While in Chiang Mai, I asked a nearby shopper for help in finding the rice, which happened to be right in front of her. Nevertheless, we talked for 10 minutes, exchanged numbers, and she invited me out to some events.

Next, **sign up for a free walking tour**. This gets you familiar with the city and allows you the opportunity to meet other travelers, though, many will only be in the city for a few days. Use this time as an opportunity to ask the guide for some additional local recommendations.

Next, buy a Hop-On/Hop-Off bus ticket. When I lived in San Francisco, I always wanted to do this, but I could never convince anyone that it was cool enough to do it with me. Or maybe it was me that was not cool enough…? Anyways, I always do this in any new city I go to. It gives me a great layout of the city and introduces me to the super-touristy things that I likely want to stay away from. This is especially useful if you plan to stay longer term and will stay in a hostel for a week before you get a more long-term accommodation, as these tours do a great job at showing you the neighborhoods—and, best of all, you'll be driving through the main streets with a bird's eye view so you can get a feel for each one within a short amount of time.

Next, **go on a pub crawl**. This will only be available in larger cities. You can look at popular hostels or on couch surfing. The crowd here is young and backpacker, but it is useful, especially on the first weekend where you don't yet know anyone to go out with.

Finally, during the time it takes me to do the previous activities, I will **search for and identify a few barbers**. I'll then choose one and book an appointment, as this makes for a great language course. Most barbers are talkative and happy to give you useful phrases using colloquial speech, local tips, upcoming events, and additional recommendations of activities and destinations. Who knows, you will sometimes even be able to befriend your barber! Plus, I find haircuts outside of the US to be economical and of the exact same quality. I have spent anywhere from $2-$15 on a haircut and beard trim from a nice establishment that includes a 10-minute neck, shoulder, and head massage.

And don't forget while you are doing all of this be extra talkative! This is your time to get out of your shell, out of your comfort zone, and gain experiences, which is 100000x better than snapping a photo on a guided tour of the touristy hot spots. You can act lost no matter where you are to ask for directions. Any question that comes to mind, and there will be many, ask someone nearby. This is going to scare the living shit out of you, especially when you do not know if the person speaks your language, if the girl/guy is really attractive, if they are a ladyboy, etc. Millions of excuses will come to mind as to why you should not talk to the stranger, but ignore all of them. Making connections will be the definitive guide in your experience.

> **TIP**
>
> While riding in tuk-tuks, rickshaws, or any non-metered transport service, I always default to handing the driver cash instead of asking how much. And I hand the driver less cash than I think it costs. I let the driver tell me if I've underpaid rather than allowing him to overcharge me. Often times, the price is known amongst locals and you identify yourself as a clueless tourist by asking the cost. You can observe this be watching when the locals exit, they always seem to know how much to pay.

10
Where To Work From

Let's face it, if you are traveling as an entrepreneur or an employee, you will be spending at least a couple hours most days of the week earning the income that supports you.

You could work from your Airbnb every day and you will get into zones when you do this for weeks at a time. However, I assure you that you will want to change up your workspace every so often. One idea you can do if you really do prefer working from home is to invite a friend you meet in your new city for a working session at your place. This may sound weird, but it is normal.

Outside of my Airbnb, my favorite workspace are cafés. I have three reasons for this preference. First, there are many more to choose from than anything else we will discuss in this chapter. Second, they are cheaper than coworking spaces. It is normal to have to buy an entire day pass at a coworking spot even if you only want to use the space for 3-4 hours. Third, it is slightly easier to meet people. This is because more people come and go, increasing your odds to start up a conversation. Plus, a café is considered a break for most people while a coworking space has more of an office feel. Three downsides of working from cafés are security, noise, and internet speed.

To counteract the noisy environment and not look like a weirdo with earplugs in, download brain.fm to use with earphones to increase focus.

Coworking spaces are great. To find them simply search 'coworking space' or go to www.coworker.com.[1] They always have strong internet, climate control, clean bathrooms, and free coffee. Another benefit is the ability to leave your laptop and go to the bathroom or even leave the space entirely, but know your laptop will still be there upon your arrival. That is not to say you cannot leave your laptop in cafés, but I know one friend who had his laptop stolen from a café in Medellin, Colombia, during his bathroom break, and I've heard many other stories.

---

1. http://www.coworker.com

My remote office setup in my Airbnb in San Jose, Costa Rica

A huge bonus of a coworking space is the amount of space you will have—usually an entire desk. This allows you to set up your additional monitor.

Coworking spaces are also great places to meet people. They also usually have weekly events that you may attend even with just a day pass purchase.

In fact, while in Mumbai, India, the manager of a coworking space I visited one day shared my number with another American who came in the day after me. Because of this, we became friends for the month I was in India. In fact, I'm sitting next to him in a coworking place right now. What a great side benefit.

CHAPTER 10

Whenever I tell someone I work from libraries, their response is always the same: "Oh! I hadn't thought of that. It's a great idea!" Why, yes, it is, thank you! They really are under-utilized. Now, it is not a place where you are likely to meet many people, but it is always free, the internet is usually fast, you are likely to find outlets easily, and the staff are always very friendly. I have actually worked in some amazing libraries around the world, and most of the time they are almost completely empty. My favorite was in Stockholm, Sweden.

One of the most beautiful libraries in Stockholm, Sweden. I turned this into my office a few days per week. Cost = $0.

An internet café is usually an option, especially in cities without libraries or coworking spots. This is not going to be your ideal option. I used this option when I was staying in a party hostel in a smaller city in Australia. It is going to be cheap with at least decent internet, but the cleanliness will be low, the chairs will be uncomfortable, and you will not have much space to work with. And you most definitely do not want to leave your computer unattended at any time.

Selina Hostels are an option in many of the larger cities. This is essentially a coworking space, but they are also an upscale hostel and have many activities to attend. The downside is many of the folks are only passing through, so you will not make many connections except if you go to the almost daily evening events, and it is going to be comparatively expensive.

I will end with my most unique recommendation: a park. The downside is that you do not have internet, unless you can turn your phone into a hotspot—or if the local parks in that city have free wi-fi, which is becoming more and more common. But this comes in handy, especially if you are writing a book, like I am in – hello, from Mumbai, India. The downside is

CHAPTER 10

you really will have to find a good location, shaded, with a comfortable chair. Or you could purchase the Share Seat I recommended in 'Chapter 7 – What To Bring' and simply find a free patch of grass, usually on a slightly downward sloping hill. Oh, and you will most definitely want to be wearing pants, or even better, bring a towel to lay down so the bugs do not tickle you and grass doesn't itch you later.

11

How To Make Friends And Connect

A recent study showed that the number one predictor for making friends was being in a high foot traffic area.

For me, and I suspect for you, the ability to make connections with people and find friends makes or breaks the experience in any destination. Am I able to connect with the locals or not?

Undoubtedly, I take this to another level. I am fanatical about making connections while I am living in a new destination. I want to build up a worldwide network of friends. Making connections touches almost every aspect of my life and I want to bring you to my frame of mind. For example, when I go to eat, I look for restaurants where I can potentially interact with other customers. I do this by looking at the seat layouts. I want a restaurant where the seating layout is such that it gives me a high chance of striking up a conversation.

I know that may seem a bit lunatic, but I find I work better if I am all in or all out—and as you might have noticed by now, I prefer to be all in. Plus, loneliness on the road is real. I want to avoid it as much as humanly possible. But most importantly, words are our most powerful tool, bar none, by far. The more I use them, the richer my life becomes. Maybe by doing this I meet a best friend, or simply a friendly person who invites me out that night. I have stories for days starting from random events like this.

Remember in your first week when you are out and about exploring the city, checking out your saved locations, and finding activities to do? Well, why not make it a point to ask locals about these things as you bump into them on the street? In addition to being scary, it is the single best thing you can do to get out of your comfort zone, which is where the magic happens. Additionally, google only functions if the locals use it. Believe it or not, many areas do not use google much. In South Korea, for example, everyone uses Naver. So those cafés you saved in your map may be just the half-decent ones the foreigners found and reviewed, while asking a person on the street could be the key to uncovering a hidden gem where you find your true love or a great friend.

Once, in the Thong Lor neighborhood in Bangkok, I stopped a man on the street to ask if the street I was walking on was the main street of Thong Lor. I knew it was, but the guy looked cool so I entered into a conversation with him. He was extremely helpful and recommended a café up the road. If I had not stopped him, I would have never found this café. It was smack next to a Starbucks, except in the back, hidden from view. I have nothing against Starbucks, but this new café, Luka Moto, was way better, more local, cheaper, with a better environment and super friendly staff.

A big one is gyms. I find that google does a terrible job (especially in smaller cities) at identifying gyms, so I always ask someone who looks fit where the good gyms are or at least what the name of the most popular gym is. Or how about where the dance studio is? Why not ask an attractive lady this question? Why not ask her to join you at one of the introduction classes? A word of caution here: While

CHAPTER 11

in Chiang Mai, Thailand, a friendly looking man approached me and asked 'Do you play chess?' I skeptically answered yes. Then he asked me if I wanted to play with him, right then and there. He actually had a set ready to go in his bag. Props to him for making the effort, but I felt the interaction was very awkward. I politely declined. I say that to say this... understand that how you say things affects the response. Do not ask for a person's time in an indefinite capacity. Make your intentions clear. In this case, it would have been wise for this guy to start off by acknowledging the awkwardness of his request by saying first: 'Excuse me, I know this is super random, but do you play chess?'

Randomly meeting strangers on the street, in the grocery store, on public transit is going to be where you make the strongest connections. It is the good old fashioned way and nothing beats it. I am dead serious. One time I was bored and feeling a bit lonely on a Friday early evening. At 6pm, I decided I will just walk around. I started a conversation with two people going home from work and we all went out that night. How awesome is that? One question I ask that almost always elicits rich responses is: What is one thing that most tourists miss that I should see?

Usually I would not recommend you go to the super touristy spots to meet people because it feels inauthentic there and you will only meet tourists leaving in a day or two. However, we can use this to our advantage, especially if you are feeling shy about approaching a stranger. When you go to places like Old Town in Tallinn, Estonia, it is only tourists (except for the locals working there), many of whom are solo or in a group of two. Depending on how long they have been traveling, especially if it is a group of two who may be slightly sick of each other, they might welcome with open arms an additional person into the group even for a day.

A study showed that the number one predictor of someone's ability to make friends was being in a high foot traffic area. So simple. When you go to touristy areas, you are simply putting yourself in a position to make friends. When I was in Ho Chi Minh, Vietnam, I decided to go to the Bitexco building where they had a lookout on the 58th floor. I know this type of activity draws mostly tourists. I wanted to do it anyways, but I realized that I could meet other tourists. I did. I met two guys who went to the same college as me and graduated the same year! We shared a beer that afternoon looking over the city and for the next two days while they were in town, we hung out. I even went to visit them in Hanoi the following week!

A great reason to start going to the gym is to meet locals. Tourists moving on a weekly basis do not go to the gym. This means your foreignness will be extremely unique, which makes it easy to start conversations. Many times a local may not want to get involved with you is because they assume you will be gone in a few days, but that is not the assumption for gym goers. I have met countless friends and lovers at the gym and even wrote an article on my strategy. You can find it on Medium: <u>How To Meet Friends + Lovers At The Gym.</u>[1]

You can use Facebook to assist you in meeting people at your new destination. Perform the following searches on Facebook to find groups and events:

- 'Digital nomad(s) [city]'
- 'Americans in[city]'
- 'Expats in [city]'
- 'Friends in [city]'

---

1. https://medium.com/@DannyBooBoo/a-strategy-to-meet-friends-lovers-at-the-gym-17f8e635c9ad

Specifically in Facebook groups, I will make a post asking if someone is willing to help me navigate the grocery store. This is only applicable if you do not know the local language. Everyone eventually goes to the grocery store and most people are more than happy helping you out one day. Or, if there is an outdoor market, I will try to form a group and we all go together. Having a local will be wise to get the local prices and to try the local snacks.

You can use MeetUp.com to find relevant groups and events. First, change your location to which city you want to see meet ups for. For smaller cities you will want to navigate to the home page and select 'All meetups'. If you are in a larger city, start with the following specific pages:

- [Expat Meetups](http://www.meetup.com/topics/expat/)[2]
- [Digital Nomad Meetups](http://www.meetup.com/topics/digital-nomads/)[3]
- [Singles Meetups](https://www.meetup.com/topics/singles/)[4]
- [Language Exchange Meetups](https://www.meetup.com/topics/language-exchange/)[5]
- [Sports Meetups](https://www.meetup.com/topics/sports/)[6]

---

2. http://www.meetup.com/topics/expat/
3. http://www.meetup.com/topics/digital-nomads/
4. https://www.meetup.com/topics/singles/
5. https://www.meetup.com/topics/language-exchange/
6. https://www.meetup.com/topics/sports/

CHAPTER 11

Regarding the language exchange events, just by the fact that you are reading this book, you are in high demand at these events. People around the world want to learn English, so you are always welcome at these events. Language exchange events can be held anywhere so you will need to consult google for this one. The best language exchange I ever attended was at a dance studio. In fact, if you want to learn the local language, think about joining a language school. They usually provide housing. If not, they almost always have weekly events. And travelers attending language school are usually staying there for at least a few weeks.

I wrote a book titled 'Zilch to Conversational: A Guide to Quickly Attain Conversational Fluency In Any Language' that I recommend you have a look at if learning languages is a passion of yours.

Here are some additional ways you can meet people in your new destination:

- Join www.Internations.org,[7] the largest network of expats. I have been to many of these events and have made some really great

---

7. http://www.Internations.org

friends. Technically an Internations group can be formed in any city, regardless of size, but in reality they are in larger cities with some exceptions. I went to an Internations event in Cali, Colombia, once with 8 people and Hong Kong with 200+ people.

- Visit www.CouchSurfing.com/events[8] for anything from language exchanges, pub crawls, sports games, and more.
  - » You can also input your travel plans even if you do not plan to use Couchsurfing for accommodations and locals will reach out to you.
- Sign up for www.NomadList.com.[9] Once here, you have access to their active Slack channel where you can easily connect with digital nomad types in all of the digital nomad hot spots plus any major destination.
  - » You can find out who you will cross paths with soon by visiting www.nomadlist.com/people[10] (ensure you are signed in)

---

8. http://www.CouchSurfing.com/events:
9. http://www.NomadList.com
10. http://www.nomadlist.com/people

CHAPTER 11

- Going to a hotel lobby or bar is a great way to spontaneously meet other travelers. The downside is that these people will only be in town for a few nights.
- Find a hostel with a pool and you can usually go enjoy it for free for the day. By default, just walk in like you are a guest and the chance someone stops you is almost zero.
- If you are near water, look for special events on boats (happy hours or boat parties).
- While eating out, request to eat at the bar where you will usually be seated by at least one other single.

12

Finding Activities

Becoming an expert in finding activities will give you great Instagram photos to make all your friends very, very jealous back home. Kidding. But it is a side benefit. This is a very important chapter because this is how you will judge the success of your time exploring the new destination. Did you go for a month and stick to your neighborhood and the touristy things (ie inauthentic)? Or did you do a bit of research, get off the beaten path a bit and find some unique activities to connect with your destination including the locals?

After this chapter, it will be the latter.

CHAPTER 12

The first thing you should do is consult google. Do a couple varied and unique searches:

- Hidden gems [destination]
  - » Replace hidden with unique, authentic, secret, undiscovered, or underrated
  - » Replace gems with attractions, things to do, spots, treasures, or activities

Then, do a few searches based on who you are and what you like to do. For example:

- Pub quiz night in [destination]
- Digital Nomad [destination]
- Stand-up comedy [destination]

While these are ok, you can usually avoid doing generic searches because all the main activities will be covered in the articles you read with the above searches. These are generic searches:

- Things to do [destination]
- Guide to [destination]

Instead, search for 'local tips [destination]'.

I will skip all the larger blogs like Frommer's, Lonely Planet, and Trip Advisor and all hotel websites like Expedia. I will do this because the best activities are usually the ones that are ranked as just ok. If you ask many people to rate an activity, you are going to get the just ok ones that do not have huge positives nor huge negatives to rank the best. They did not do anything wrong, but they also did not do anything special. It is your job to seek out a wide variety of activities and decide how awesome it will be for you individually, not for the 70-year old grandma.

Additionally, the recommendations here are static. You are not going to get the new thing to do as of this or last year. The only things that make these big websites are the absolute most touristy things you could possibly do (i.e. the very things you generally avoid like the plague in your home city).

In your searches, you want to focus on the second, third, and fourth pages. This is where you will get more authentic bloggers just sharing their experience for no other reason that because they want to. Plus, you will also get the above super touristy destinations by default and you can select which of these you find interesting and may want to visit during your time exploring your new destination.

CHAPTER 12

One of the most unique guides that I have ever found is [Atlas Obscura](https://www.atlasobscura.com/).[1] Their tagline is 'Curious and Wonderous Travel Destinations.' I will almost always add at least a few unique things to do in each city I am in to this website.

Sofar Sounds are expanding to new cities quickly. They are a secret and intimate musical gig where 3–4 performers play sets for the small audience. The focus of the gathering is the music, so it's a much different experience than heading to a neighborhood bar where a band is playing and glasses are clinking. For music fans, this is a unique way to support small artists while meeting like-minded people who savor live music.

Give Pinterest a try. Just search for your destination city and a bunch of relevant and useful information will pop up. Bonus: you will find neighborhood guides here, too.

Download the app [Showaround](https://www.showaround.com/).[2] It is super simple. Enter your dates of travel and destination and locals will reach out to you with things to do. About 50% will be free and the other 50% will cost money, usu-

---

1. https://www.atlasobscura.com/
2. https://www.showaround.com/

Finding Activities

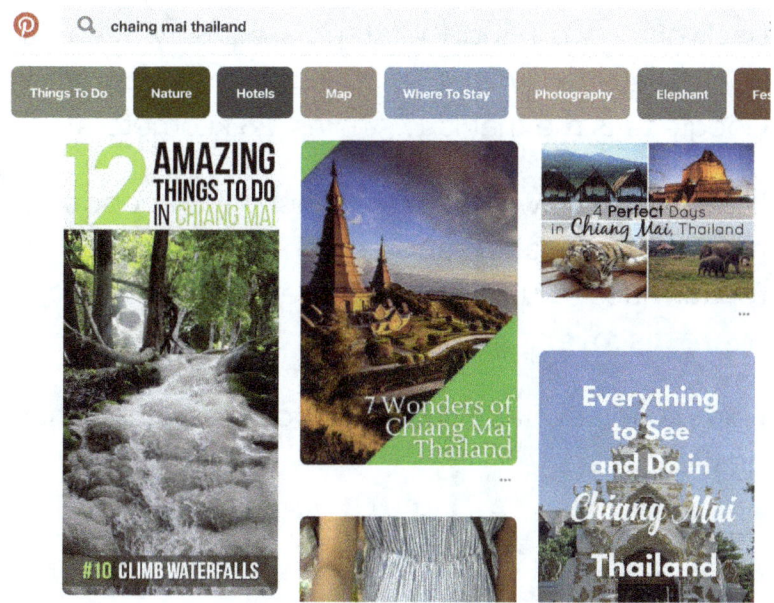

The search results on Pinterest for 'chiang mai thailand'

ally between $2-$8 per hour. I have done this a few times and these people—they are not professional tour operators, just regular locals—usually become your friends during your time there.

While you were researching the neighborhoods, make note of the ones you did not choose and take an afternoon or evening to explore them. I simply walk on the main avenue and then get lost from there. I recommend you download a walking app like Google Fit[3] to measure your steps. It is neat to look

---

3. https://www.google.com/fit/

back on it and I find the steps are pretty accurate. Some days I have taken more than 35,000 steps. Google tells me that is 17.5 miles (28 kilometers).

Upon arrival, I will change my city in Facebook to my new destination and search the coming week for activities. You can find this feature at [Facebook's event discovery section](http://www.facebook.com/events/discovery).[4]

Here is a list of activities that you will find in most destinations:

- Zoo
- Amusement park
- Beaches
- Parks (there is nothing nicer than taking a nap under a tree at 2pm in 75F (24C) degree weather. This is freedom!)
- Shopping centers
- Outdoor markets (seafood, flowers, electronics, clothes, etc.)
- Bike tour
- Local food or coffee or alcohol tours
- Yoga

---

4. http://www.facebook.com/events/discovery

In many cities (and many cities every month), you can find a bunch of [Airbnb Experiences](#).[5] These are supposed to be unique. At the time of this writing, this is still very new so that you can make a reservation today for today or tomorrow and you are likely to be the only person on the experience, unless maybe it is the most popular one or two in the area. I recommend doing an activity like this early on in your trip as the tour guide as a local can give you unrelated (to the Airbnb Experience) tips about your new destination. I have even hung out with many of these guides in the days after the Experience. You will find they are broken down into categories.

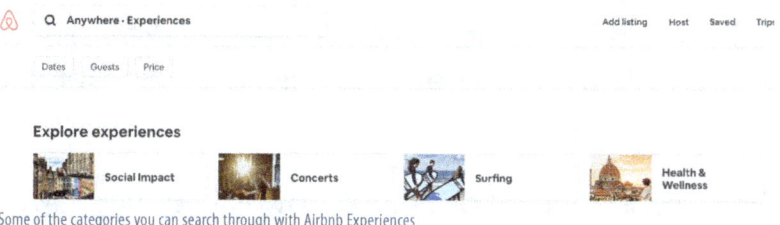

Some of the categories you can search through with Airbnb Experiences

Similar to Airbnb Experiences is the app [Withlocals](#).[6]

Remember when I said you need to research what that city is known for so that you can connect yourself

---

5. https://www.airbnb.com/s/experiences
6. https://www.withlocals.com/

CHAPTER 12

more strongly with the destination? Well, it will give you some great activities to do. In Pereira, Colombia, where they make the best coffee in the world, you can go into the mountains to explore a coffee farm. Or in Mexico City, where they are famous for their Luchas, go to a wrestling match. Or maybe the city is known for a type of liquor and you can tour the facility in your destination. Why not take advantage of this!?!

Or, just in general, what activities do you enjoy? List them all out and some are bound to be options in your new cities. Stand-up comedy? Break dancing? Movie buff? Literature buff? Karaoke buff? I love basketball. I happen to be pretty good and this becomes a place where I easily make friends. In all destinations I keep my eyes out for basketball courts.

For all you foodies out there, now is your time! Myself, I am no foodie. I cook most of my meals and seeking out food in my destination for whatever reason does not interest me. When I hear of something cool, I will mark it down. The other day I heard of an all-you-can-eat buffet at a fancy hotel for only 290Bhat ($9). It is new, so it still has the intro deal going and it is not yet known. Anyways, here are a few websites you can find locals to eat with or cook you food. I find that neither is a leader, instead some have meals in each destination while others do not:

- [Eatwith][7]
- [Meal Sharing][8]
- [Eataway][9]

Try to find local holidays, festivals, concerts, fairs, celebrations in your destination city. When I was in Chiang Mai, I happened to be there for the Loi Krathong Festival. You will know what this is with my photo. If I had stayed a few months longer, I would have been there for the Songkran Festival, a three-day event with water guns, water balloons, buckets of water.

Loi Krathong festival in Chiang Mai, Thailand

---

7. https://www.eatwith.com/
8. https://www.mealsharing.com
9. https://www.eataway.com/

CHAPTER 12

Sometimes I will search Instagram or Twitter for the destination including locations, relevant hashtags (for example, #mydubai in Dubai or #calico in Cali, Colombia), and accounts. This often times does present some additional activities, but it is hit or miss. Sometimes I simply learn some useful information or about a neat restaurant or bar I want to check out.

You can search the most popular hostels website for organized activities. Even if there is something you want to do, but are not sure about transportation, sometimes you can join the transport with a hostel tour.

If you happen to know the local language, search Facebook for local groups in the target language. As an example of a local group, I found one called the Bondi Bubble in Bondi Beach, Sydney, Australia. As a group of only locals (tourists likely do not know the term the locals use to signify that people who live in this area usually do not leave often), I found it tremendously helpful.

Now, if you just want to interact with tourists or people who speak English, then find the most touristy bar and go. I find it is easier to go to these places solo and make friends as it is so touristy. For example, when I was in Casablanca, I went to Rick's Café, a bar designed to recreate the bar made famous in the movie Casablanca (which was not even filmed in Casablanca, by the way!).

I find that often times without a regular 9-5 if you are a traveling entrepreneur, or in your free and unplanned days if you are a vacationer, there will be times when you become bored. Remember that feeling? You will actually sit down and realize you have no real pressing time commitments. It's 2 o'clock and you figure you might as well enjoy the day. Here is a list of 2-4 hour activities you can do without much planning:

- Go to a café to read or people watch
    » You can also go to a new coworking spot just to check it out, a library, or Selina
- Go to a yoga class
- Find a hostel with a pool and hang out there
- Get a massage
- Go to the tourist information center
- Common activities: hop-on/off bus, zoo, walking tour, theme parks
- Go to a beach or park
- Explore a neighborhood
    » Simply walk on the main street and window shop
- Visit a new shopping center or outdoor market

- Play basketball (or your personal activity)
- Browse in a bookstore
- Check Facebook Events
- Go to an upscale hotel lobby or bar
- Couchsurfing Hangouts
  - » Within the app, free travelers identify themselves if they are available to hang out right now and they also list what they want to do

13
How To Take Full Advantage Of Your Life

In general and no matter what you are currently doing with your life, you should be asking yourself how you can take full advantage of your current situation.

Our current situation is traveling the world and exploring new destinations while making new connections with people. But is there more? Can we more fully take advantage of our situations? Yes!

I am going to show you how I try to take full advantage of my situation in the hope that it will give you ideas about your own.

If you are already traveling to a destination, step number one is figuring out what it is known or famous for. We already discussed the merits of this.

CHAPTER 13

A certain place may be famous for something you had no idea about, but are actually interested in. For example, say you are going to Milan, Italy, and did not know it is the fashion capital of the world. You happen to be interested in fashion, so now you plan out exactly where you live and maybe you can take a fashion design seminar, something you could not do in your own town.

Did you know that Turkey is world-famous for hair transplants? If you were going bald, this might unexpectedly surprise and excite you.

I will be traveling to Georgia (the country in Europe) later this year explicitly to open a European bank account, and Georgian bank accounts return about 10% interest.

Take note of your own hobbies. Mine are basketball, weight-lifting, and counting cards. This is how I apply each of my hobbies to my traveling:

- Weight-lifting — The only thing in life I consider myself addicted to is lifting heavy weight. Well, there happens to be a professional industry dedicated to this. So why not schedule some of my travels to go to fitness industry conferences? Or go workout at gyms around the world with professional bodybuilding teams? For example, Oxygen Gym in Kuwait is home to many professional bodybuilders like Big Ramy. Wouldn't it be cool to train with them?

- Basketball — I love playing basketball. It is my cardio and how I make friends, so I have built a list on my computer of countries in the world who love basketball. Some are obvious, but did you know the number one sport in the Philippines is basketball?
- Counting Cards — I love casinos. I enjoy the atmosphere, the energy, everything. I also love the strategy of Blackjack and counting cards, but counting cards is grounds to get kicked out of a casino for life (though not illegal). So if I happen to be in a city with a casino, I will make a few stops there to have some fun.

Monkeys are my favorite animal and so I have a list of destinations around the world with monkey habitats or zoos. If I get close to these destinations, I decide if I want to make an extra stop there. Right now, as I write this, I am in Bali, Indonesia, where there are two monkey forests nearby.

How about soon-to-be-hobbies? Goals you have? Or skills you want to acquire? For example, I want

CHAPTER 13

to learn how to play the drums, become a pilot, and improve my massaging skills. I am sure there are certain cities on this planet that are more ideal for learning drums, piloting, and massaging. Eventually, I will do these searches and go to wherever is most efficient for me to learn this new skill.

I also am pretty active on Instagram so I try to take advantage of the fact that I am exploring new destinations by taking good photos and uploading them on a regular basis. I will usually search for the most Instagrammable spots in my destination and take a trip out there during some free time, ideally with a local friend I made, and take some photos and explore the area.

If you do not already have a bucket list, I recommend you create one. This way you can do a few really awesome and special things when you are already in the area anyways.

Obviously, if you can take advantage in any way to help your business, that makes a lot of sense. For me, I will do a search of 'Airbnb property management' in any new city I am in to meet with businesses. This is something I do as part of growing my business. I am already in a foreign land, why not make it help my business in any way possible? I will also look for Airbnb clubs and will let them know I am in town and happy to come to a meeting, which often leads to speaking engagements.

Lastly, how about some conferences that you are interested in attending? You can create your travel plans to sync with an upcoming conference you have. I decided to leave Latin America and explore Asia because a group I joined that year, Dynamite Circle, had their annual conference in Bangkok, Thailand. Because of that conference, I learned of a seminar held only once per year for a group of five people in South Korea titled 'The Art and Science of Sex' which I decided to attend. The year prior, I worked into my travel plans to attend a 3-day persuasion seminar with 3 other students held in Toronto, Canada.

I also mentioned the dance cruise, Aventura, and the cruise for digital nomads, Nomad Cruise. These are both things I am sure I'll modify my travel plans around in the near future.

14
Checklist: Putting It All Together

Below is a culmination of all the 'to-dos' that you would do related to your new destination. While it is an exhaustive list, you will not need to do everything in every place. And while most of this is generic and will be applicable to you, I wanted to add in the specifics to me to present a real-life example (you probably won't search for Airbnb property management companies in each city, for example). Here goes:

a. Google searches to learn about new destinations
   i. Interesting facts [destination]
   ii. Local tips [destination]
   iii. Hidden gems [destination]
   - Replace hidden with unique, authentic, secret, undiscovered, or underrated

- Replace gems with attractions, things to do, spots, treasures, or activities
        iv. Digital Nomad [destination]
        v. What is [destination] famous/known for
        vi. Most Instagrammable spots [destination]
        vii. Airbnb property management [destination]
        viii. Find local holidays, festivals, concerts, fairs, celebrations
    b. Searching other services to find activities:
        i. [Atlas Obscura][1]
        ii. [Pinterest][2]
        iii. [Airbnb Experiences][3]
        iv. [Couchsurfing Events][4]
        v. [Facebook Events][5]
        vi. [Internations][6]
        vii. [Nomad List Events][7]
        viii. [Yelp Events][8]
        ix. [Withlocals][9]

---

1. https://www.atlasobscura.com/
2. http://Pinterest
3. https://www.airbnb.com/s/experiences
4. http://www.CouchSurfing.com/events
5. http://www.facebook.com/events/discovery
6. https://www.internations.org
7. http://www.facebook.com/pg/nomadlist/events/
8. http://www.yelp.com/events
9. https://www.withlocals.com/

c. Create language deck in Anki with common words and phrases
d. Connect with people
   i. [Showaround](https://www.showaround.com/)[10]
   ii. [Couchsurfing Hangouts](http://Couchsurfing)[11]
      • Input your travel itinerary
   iii. [Nomad List People](http://www.nomadlist.com/people)[12]
e. Join Facebook groups
   i. Digital nomad(s) [city]
   ii. Americans in[city]
   iii. Expats in [city]
   iv. Friends in [city]
   v. Salsa/Latin dance [city]
   vi. Language Exchange [city]
   vii. Improve [city]
   viii. Ask Facebook groups for local, competitive basketball games
f. Join meetup groups
   i. [Expat Meetups](http://www.meetup.com/topics/expat/)[13]
   ii. [Digital Nomad Meetups](http://www.meetup.com/topics/digital-nomads/)[14]

---

10. https://www.showaround.com/
11. http://Couchsurfing
12. http://www.nomadlist.com/people
13. http://www.meetup.com/topics/expat/
14. http://www.meetup.com/topics/digital-nomads/

    iii. [Singles Meetups](#)[15]
    iv. [Language Exchange Meetups](#)[16]
    v. [Sports Meetups](#)[17]
g. Download offline map of your city
    i. Also download the location language onto your google translate app.
h. Change city on social media accounts
    i. Facebook, meetup, couchsurfing, internations, coffee meets bagel, nomadlist.
i. Upon arrival, search for things one by one. I wait until arrival because I can order by distance from a certain location on my phone map.
    i. Gym (search also health club, or fitness club)
    ii. Café (or coffee shop)
    iii. Library and coworking locations
    iv. Grocery store (search also supermarket)
    v. Shopping Center
    vi. Parks or beaches
    vii. Comedy or improv clubs
    viii. Jazz clubs
    ix. Basketball courts

---

15. http://www.meetup.com/topics/singles/
16. http://www.meetup.com/topics/language-exchange/
17. http://www.meetup.com/topics/sports/

j. General activities
    i. Search Instagram for relevant and local hashtags or accounts
    ii. Pub crawl
    iii. Hop on/hop off bus
    iv. Weekly events at coworking spaces or hostels
    v. Walking or biking tour
    vi. Tourist Center
    vii. Hotel lobby or bar
    viii. Hostel with pool/café
    ix. Zoo
    x. Amusement/water park

Again, here is a list of 2-4 hour activities you can do without much planning:

- Go to a café to read or people watch
  - » You can also go to a new coworking spot just to check it out, a library, or Selina
- Go to a yoga class
- Find a hostel with a pool and hang out there
- Get a massage
- Go to the tourist information center
- Common activities: hop-on/off bus, zoo, walking tour, theme parks

- Go to a beach or park
- Explore a neighborhood
  - » Simply walk on the main street and window shop
- Visit a new shopping center or outdoor market
- Play basketball (or your personal activity)
- Browse in a bookstore
- Check Facebook Events
- Go to an upscale hotel lobby or bar

15
List Of Resources

[Airbnb Experiences](#) – Unique activities in select cities

[Atlas Obscura](#) – "Curious and Wondrous Travel Destinations"

[Couchsurfing Hangouts](#) – a way to meet other travelers, typically backpackers

[Cruise Sheet](#) – cruise deal alerts

[Earth Class Mail](#) – mail scanning, forwarding, and virtual address service

[Eataway](#) – A worldwide community of local cooks offering great home-cooked meals

[Eatwith](#) – "Food Experiences With Locals Around The World"

[Facebook Events](#) – Easy, straight-forward way to find activities in your city

CHAPTER 15

[Flystein](#) – paid service where the experts will search for a flight on your behalf

[GeoBlue](#) – full coverage international health insurance that I use and recommend

[Google Fit](#) – Phone app to track your steps

[Meal Sharing](#) – "Eat with people from around the world."

[Nomad List Events](#) – Facebook events for the digital nomad types, limited availability

[Nomad Soulmate Events](#) – think Tinder for digital nomads

[Scott's Cheap Flights](#) – paid user-friendly website that shows you cheap flights based on your selected airports

[Sofar Sounds](#) – Secret gigs and intimate concerts

[Showaround](#) – "Find a Local to Show You Around"

[TransferWise](#) – easiest for transferring money from US bank to a foreign bank

[Travel Hacking Cartel](#) – paid resource to earn extra mileage points

[Withlocals](#) – Enjoy a city like a local - unique things to do, private tours …

[World Nomads](#) – international health coverage

16
Time To Begin

Ok. I hope I have prepared you for your upcoming epic experiences. I just want to leave you with one final note. During your travels, keep track of and identify why you liked or disliked a particular destination. Do so by creating a list of characteristics of your ideal city in terms of priority. This will help you get to know yourself and help guide you in the future to where you may want to visit.

Here's my list in order of importance of what I value in a destination. Over the years, it has gotten extremely detailed so I know exactly which cities I will and won't like. I attach a score of 0, 0.5, or 1 to each category of each city. Some of these are subjective, but where I have quantitative metrics, I say so. Essentially, you are creating your own **Mercer Quality of Living Index**,[1] only difference is it is 100% personalized to you.

---

1. https://en.wikipedia.org/wiki/Mercer_Quality_of_Living_Survey

CHAPTER 16

These are the 18 categories by importance I use to judge cities:

1. Climate
   - A score of 1 is awarded to any city that has an average daily temperature of at least 18C/68F and less than 40mm/1.6inch rain per month.
2. Cost of living
   - A score of 1 is awarded to a city with a cost of living less than $1,000 per month, excluding housing.
3. Attractive women
   - Subjective and based on my observations during the daytime as I don't go out a lot at night.
4. Quantity of gyms
   - Generally cities fall into one of three categories: many quality gyms nearby, one quality gym nearby, zero quality gyms.
5. Walkability
6. Air pollution
   - A score of 1 is awarded to a city which an AQI of less than 50.

7. Friendly locals
8. Transit
   - A score of 1 is awarded to a city with very little traffic or the ability to bypass traffic (for example, with a scooter).
9. Many cafes
10. Nightlife
    - A score of 1 is awarded to a city where the bars close before 1am. I like nightlife to end early because that means it starts early. I'm not one to party until 4am.
11. Expat events
12. Not religious
    - A score of 1 is awarded to a city where more than 75% of the population says religion is not important.
13. Day trips
    - A score of 1 is awarded to a city where there are at least 5 day or weekend trips within a 4 hour travel radius of the city.
14. Prostitution
15. Basketball community
16. Salsa community

CHAPTER 16

17. Beach
    - A score of 1 is awarded to a city where the beach is within a 15-minute drive from the city center.
18. Cleanliness (i.e. no trash on the streets and locals don't throw garbage on the street)

I only rank the cities that I know will score the best. For me and based on the above list, Chiang Mai, Thailand ranks number one in the world with a score of 11.5.

How'd I do? I hope you got tremendous value out of this book. Please do consider leaving a review.

Connect With Me

Let's meet in an upcoming destination. I update my personal website with where I will be over the next few months. You can find more information at www.dannybooboo.com.

Or connect with me on Instagram: @DannyBooBoo0

You can also find me on Facebook as Daniel Vroman Rusteen.

Or subscribe to my YouTube channel by searching 'dannybooboo'.

Happy travels!

www.ingramcontent.com/pod-product-compliance
Lightning Source LLC
Chambersburg PA
CBHW070432010526
44118CB00014B/2007